this notebook belongs to

DATE _____ m t w t f s s

Today I'M thankful for

1 _____
2 _____
3 _____

Something awesome that happened today

My level of happiness

DATE _____ m t w t f s s

Today I'M thankful for

1 _____
2 _____
3 _____

Something awesome that happened today

My level of happiness

DATE _____ m t w t f s s

Today I'M thankful for

1 _____
2 _____
3 _____

Something awesome that happened today

_____
_____
_____
_____
_____
_____
_____
_____
_____

My level of happiness

DATE _____ m t w t f s s

Today I'M thankful for

1. _____
2. _____
3. _____

Something awesome that happened today

My level of happiness

DATE _____ m t w t f s s

Today I'M thankful for

1. _____
2. _____
3. _____

Something awesome that happened today

My level of happiness

DATE _____ m t w t f s s

Today I'M thankful for

1 _____
2 _____
3 _____

Something awesome that happened today

_____
_____
_____
_____
_____
_____
_____
_____
_____

My level of happiness

DATE _____ m t w t f s s

Today I'M thankful for

1 _____
2 _____
3 _____

Something awesome that happened today

My level of happiness

DATE _____ m t w t f s s

Today I'M thankful for

1 _____
2 _____
3 _____

Something awesome that happened today

My level of happiness

DATE _____ m t w t f s s

Today I'M thankful for

1. _____
2. _____
3. _____

Something awesome that happened today

My level of happiness

DATE _____ m t w t f s s

Today I'M thankful for

1. _____
2. _____
3. _____

Something awesome that happened today

My level of happiness

DATE _____ m t w t f s s

Today I'M thankful for

1 _____
2 _____
3 _____

Something awesome that happened today

_____
_____
_____
_____
_____
_____
_____
_____
_____
_____

My level of happiness

DATE _____ m t w t f s s

Today I'M thankful for

1 _____
2 _____
3 _____

Something awesome that happened today

My level of happiness

DATE _____ m t w t f s s

Today I'M thankful for

1 _____
2 _____
3 _____

Something awesome that happened today

My level of happiness

DATE _____ m t w t f s s

Today I'M thankful for

1 _____
2 _____
3 _____

Something awesome that happened today

_____
_____
_____
_____
_____
_____
_____
_____

My level of happiness

DATE _____ m t w t f s s

Today I'M thankful for

1 _____
2 _____
3 _____

Something awesome that happened today

_____
_____
_____
_____
_____
_____
_____
_____
_____
_____

My level of happiness

DATE _____ m t w t f s s

Today I'M thankful for

1. _____
2. _____
3. _____

Something awesome that happened today

_____
_____
_____
_____
_____
_____
_____
_____

My level of happiness

DATE _____ m t w t f s s

Today I'M thankful for

1 _____
2 _____
3 _____

Something awesome that happened today

My level of happiness

DATE _____ m t w t f s s

Today I'M thankful for

1 _____
2 _____
3 _____

Something awesome that happened today

My level of happiness

DATE _____ m t w t f s s

Today I'M thankful for

1. _____
2. _____
3. _____

Something awesome that happened today

My level of happiness

DATE _____ m t w t f s s

Today I'M thankful for

1. _____
2. _____
3. _____

Something awesome that happened today

My level of happiness

DATE _____ m t w t f s s

Today I'M thankful for

1 _____
2 _____
3 _____

Something awesome that happened today

My level of happiness

DATE _____ m t w t f s s

Today I'M thankful for

1. _____
2. _____
3. _____

Something awesome that happened today

My level of happiness

DATE _____ m t w t f s s

Today I'M thankful for

1 _____
2 _____
3 _____

Something awesome that happened today

My level of happiness

DATE _____ m t w t f s s

Today I'M thankful for

1. _____
2. _____
3. _____

Something awesome that happened today

My level of happiness

DATE _____ m t w t f s s

Today I'M thankful for

1. _____
2. _____
3. _____

Something awesome that happened today

My level of happiness

DATE _____ m t w t f s s

Today I'M thankful for

1 _____
2 _____
3 _____

Something awesome that happened today

My level of happiness

DATE _____ m t w t f s s

Today I'M thankful for

1. _____
2. _____
3. _____

Something awesome that happened today

_____
_____
_____
_____
_____
_____
_____
_____
_____

My level of happiness

DATE _____ m t w t f s s

Today I'M thankful for

1. _____
2. _____
3. _____

Something awesome that happened today

My level of happiness

DATE _____ m t w t f s s

Today I'M thankful for

1 _____
2 _____
3 _____

Something awesome that happened today

_____
_____
_____
_____
_____
_____
_____
_____
_____

My level of happiness

DATE _____ m t w t f s s

Today I'M thankful for

1 _____
2 _____
3 _____

Something awesome that happened today

My level of happiness

DATE _____ m t w t f s s

Today I'M thankful for

1 _____
2 _____
3 _____

Something awesome that happened today

_____
_____
_____
_____
_____
_____
_____
_____
_____

My level of happiness

DATE _____ m t w t f s s

Today I'M thankful for

1. _____
2. _____
3. _____

Something awesome that happened today

My level of happiness

DATE _____ m t w t f s s

Today I'M thankful for

1. _____
2. _____
3. _____

Something awesome that happened today

_____
_____
_____
_____
_____
_____
_____
_____

My level of happiness

DATE _____ m t w t f s s

Today I'M thankful for

1 _____
2 _____
3 _____

Something awesome that happened today

My level of happiness

DATE _____ m t w t f s s

Today I'M thankful for

1 _____
2 _____
3 _____

Something awesome that happened today

My level of happiness

DATE _____ m t w t f s s

Today I'M thankful for

1 _____
2 _____
3 _____

Something awesome that happened today

My level of happiness

DATE _____ m t w t f s s

Today I'M thankful for

1 _____
2 _____
3 _____

Something awesome that happened today

My level of happiness

DATE _____ m t w t f s s

Today I'M thankful for

1. _____
2. _____
3. _____

Something awesome that happened today

My level of happiness

DATE _____ m t w t f s s

Today I'M thankful for

1 _____
2 _____
3 _____

Something awesome that happened today

_____
_____
_____
_____
_____
_____
_____
_____
_____

My level of happiness

DATE _____ m t w t f s s

Today I'M thankful for

1 _____
2 _____
3 _____

Something awesome that happened today

My level of happiness

DATE _____ m t w t f s s

Today I'M thankful for

1. _____
2. _____
3. _____

Something awesome that happened today

My level of happiness

DATE _____ m t w t f s s

Today I'M thankful for

1. _____
2. _____
3. _____

Something awesome that happened today

My level of happiness

DATE _____   m t w t f s s

Today I'M thankful for

1. _____
2. _____
3. _____

Something awesome that happened today

_____

My level of happiness

DATE _____ m t w t f s s

Today I'M thankful for

1. _____
2. _____
3. _____

Something awesome that happened today

My level of happiness

DATE _____ m t w t f s s

Today I'M thankful for

1. _____
2. _____
3. _____

Something awesome that happened today

My level of happiness

DATE _____ m t w t f s s

Today I'M thankful for

1. _____
2. _____
3. _____

Something awesome that happened today

My level of happiness

DATE _____ m t w t f s s

Today I'M thankful for

1 _____
2 _____
3 _____

Something awesome that happened today

My level of happiness

DATE _____ m t w t f s s

Today I'M thankful for

1 _____
2 _____
3 _____

Something awesome that happened today

_____
_____
_____
_____
_____
_____
_____
_____

My level of happiness

DATE _____ m t w t f s s

Today I'M thankful for

1 _____
2 _____
3 _____

Something awesome that happened today

My level of happiness

DATE _____ m t w t f s s

Today I'M thankful for

1 _____
2 _____
3 _____

Something awesome that happened today

My level of happiness

DATE _____ m t w t f s s

Today I'M thankful for

1 _____
2 _____
3 _____

Something awesome that happened today

My level of happiness

DATE _____ m t w t f s s

Today I'M thankful for

1. _____
2. _____
3. _____

Something awesome that happened today

My level of happiness

DATE _____ m t w t f s s

Today I'M thankful for

1 _____
2 _____
3 _____

Something awesome that happened today

My level of happiness

DATE _____ m t w t f s s

Today I'M thankful for

1 _____
2 _____
3 _____

Something awesome that happened today

_____
_____
_____
_____
_____
_____
_____
_____
_____

My level of happiness

DATE _____ m t w t f s s

Today I'M thankful for

1 _____
2 _____
3 _____

Something awesome that happened today

My level of happiness

DATE _____ m t w t f s s

Today I'M thankful for

1 _____
2 _____
3 _____

Something awesome that happened today

_____
_____
_____
_____
_____
_____
_____
_____
_____

My level of happiness

DATE _____ m t w t f s s

Today I'M thankful for

1. _____
2. _____
3. _____

Something awesome that happened today

_____
_____
_____
_____
_____
_____
_____
_____
_____

My level of happiness

DATE _____ m t w t f s s

Today I'M thankful for

1. _____
2. _____
3. _____

Something awesome that happened today

_____
_____
_____
_____
_____
_____
_____
_____
_____

My level of happiness

DATE _____ m t w t f s s

Today I'M thankful for

1. _____
2. _____
3. _____

Something awesome that happened today

My level of happiness

DATE _____ m t w t f s s

Today I'M thankful for

1. _____
2. _____
3. _____

Something awesome that happened today

My level of happiness

DATE _____ m t w t f s s

Today I'M thankful for

1. _____
2. _____
3. _____

Something awesome that happened today

_____
_____
_____
_____
_____
_____
_____
_____

My level of happiness

DATE _____ m t w t f s s

Today I'M thankful for

1. _____
2. _____
3. _____

Something awesome that happened today

_____
_____
_____
_____
_____
_____
_____
_____
_____

My level of happiness

DATE _____ m t w t f s s

Today I'M thankful for

1 _____
2 _____
3 _____

Something awesome that happened today

_____
_____
_____
_____
_____
_____
_____
_____
_____
_____

My level of happiness

DATE _____ m t w t f s s

Today I'M thankful for

1. _____
2. _____
3. _____

Something awesome that happened today

_____
_____
_____
_____
_____
_____
_____
_____
_____
_____

My level of happiness

DATE _____ m t w t f s s

Today I'M thankful for

1 _____
2 _____
3 _____

Something awesome that happened today

_____
_____
_____
_____
_____
_____
_____
_____
_____

My level of happiness

DATE _____ m t w t f s s

Today I'M thankful for

1 _____
2 _____
3 _____

Something awesome that happened today

My level of happiness

DATE _____ m t w t f s s

Today I'M thankful for

1 _____
2 _____
3 _____

Something awesome that happened today

My level of happiness

DATE _____ m t w t f s s

Today I'M thankful for

1. _____
2. _____
3. _____

Something awesome that happened today

My level of happiness

DATE _____ m t w t f s s

Today I'M thankful for

1 _____
2 _____
3 _____

Something awesome that happened today

My level of happiness

DATE _____ m t w t f s s

Today I'M thankful for

1. _____
2. _____
3. _____

Something awesome that happened today

My level of happiness

DATE _____ m t w t f s s

Today I'M thankful for

1. _____
2. _____
3. _____

Something awesome that happened today

My level of happiness

DATE _____ m t w t f s s

Today I'M thankful for

1 _____
2 _____
3 _____

Something awesome that happened today

_____
_____
_____
_____
_____
_____
_____
_____

My level of happiness

DATE _____ m t w t f s s

Today I'M thankful for

1. _____
2. _____
3. _____

Something awesome that happened today

My level of happiness

DATE _____ m t w t f s s

Today I'M thankful for

1. _____
2. _____
3. _____

Something awesome that happened today

_____
_____
_____
_____
_____
_____
_____
_____

My level of happiness

DATE _____ m t w t f s s

Today I'M thankful for

1. _____
2. _____
3. _____

Something awesome that happened today

_____
_____
_____
_____
_____
_____
_____
_____
_____

My level of happiness

DATE _____ m t w t f s s

Today I'M thankful for

1 _____
2 _____
3 _____

Something awesome that happened today

My level of happiness

DATE _____ m t w t f s s

Today I'M thankful for

1 _____
2 _____
3 _____

Something awesome that happened today

_____
_____
_____
_____
_____
_____
_____
_____
_____

My level of happiness

DATE _____ m t w t f s s

Today I'M thankful for

1 _____
2 _____
3 _____

Something awesome that happened today

My level of happiness

DATE _____ m t w t f s s

Today I'M thankful for

1 _____
2 _____
3 _____

Something awesome that happened today

_____
_____
_____
_____
_____
_____
_____
_____
_____

My level of happiness

DATE _____ m t w t f s s

Today I'M thankful for

1 _____
2 _____
3 _____

Something awesome that happened today

My level of happiness

DATE _____ m t w t f s s

Today I'M thankful for

1 _____
2 _____
3 _____

Something awesome that happened today

My level of happiness

DATE _____ m t w t f s s

Today I'M thankful for

1. _____
2. _____
3. _____

Something awesome that happened today

My level of happiness

DATE _____ m t w t f s s

Today I'M thankful for

1. _____
2. _____
3. _____

Something awesome that happened today

My level of happiness

DATE _____ m t w t f s s

Today I'M thankful for

1. _____
2. _____
3. _____

Something awesome that happened today

My level of happiness

DATE _____ m t w t f s s

Today I'M thankful for

1 _____
2 _____
3 _____

Something awesome that happened today

My level of happiness

DATE _____ m t w t f s s

Today I'M thankful for

1. _____
2. _____
3. _____

Something awesome that happened today

My level of happiness

DATE _____ m t w t f s s

Today I'M thankful for

1 _____
2 _____
3 _____

Something awesome that happened today

My level of happiness

DATE _____ m t w t f s s

Today I'M thankful for

1 _____
2 _____
3 _____

Something awesome that happened today

My level of happiness

DATE _____ m t w t f s s

Today I'M thankful for

1 _____
2 _____
3 _____

Something awesome that happened today

My level of happiness

DATE _____ m t w t f s s

Today I'M thankful for

1 _____
2 _____
3 _____

Something awesome that happened today

My level of happiness

DATE _____ m t w t f s s

Today I'M thankful for

1. _____
2. _____
3. _____

Something awesome that happened today

My level of happiness

DATE _____ m t w t f s s

Today I'M thankful for

1. _____
2. _____
3. _____

Something awesome that happened today

My level of happiness

DATE _____ m t w t f s s

Today I'M thankful for

1. _____
2. _____
3. _____

Something awesome that happened today

My level of happiness

DATE _____ m t w t f s s

Today I'M thankful for

1. _____
2. _____
3. _____

Something awesome that happened today

My level of happiness

DATE _____ m t w t f s s

Today I'M thankful for

1 _____
2 _____
3 _____

Something awesome that happened today

My level of happiness

DATE _____ m t w t f s s

Today I'M thankful for

1. _____
2. _____
3. _____

Something awesome that happened today

My level of happiness

DATE _____ m t w t f s s

Today I'M thankful for

1. _____
2. _____
3. _____

Something awesome that happened today

_____
_____
_____
_____
_____
_____
_____
_____

My level of happiness

DATE _____ m t w t f s s

Today I'M thankful for

1 _____
2 _____
3 _____

Something awesome that happened today

My level of happiness

DATE _____ m t w t f s s

Today I'M thankful for

1. _____
2. _____
3. _____

Something awesome that happened today

My level of happiness

DATE _____ m t w t f s s

Today I'M thankful for

1. _____
2. _____
3. _____

Something awesome that happened today

_____
_____
_____
_____
_____
_____
_____
_____
_____

My level of happiness

DATE _____ m t w t f s s

Today I'M thankful for

1. _____
2. _____
3. _____

Something awesome that happened today

_____
_____
_____
_____
_____
_____
_____
_____
_____

My level of happiness

DATE _____ m t w t f s s

Today I'M thankful for

1. _____
2. _____
3. _____

Something awesome that happened today

My level of happiness

DATE _____ m t w t f s s

Today I'M thankful for

1 _____
2 _____
3 _____

Something awesome that happened today

My level of happiness

DATE _____ m t w t f s s

Today I'M thankful for

1. _____
2. _____
3. _____

Something awesome that happened today

My level of happiness

DATE _____ m t w t f s s

Today I'M thankful for

1 _____
2 _____
3 _____

Something awesome that happened today

My level of happiness

DATE _____ m t w t f s s

Today I'M thankful for

1 _____
2 _____
3 _____

Something awesome that happened today

My level of happiness

DATE _____ m t w t f s s

Today I'M thankful for

1 _____
2 _____
3 _____

Something awesome that happened today

My level of happiness

DATE _____ m t w t f s s

Today I'M thankful for

1. _____
2. _____
3. _____

Something awesome that happened today

_____
_____
_____
_____
_____
_____
_____
_____

My level of happiness

Copyright © 2019
All rights reserved. No part of this publication may be reproduced, distributed, or transmitted in any form or by any means, including photocopying, recording, or other electronic or mechanical methods, without the prior written permission of the publisher, except in the case of brief quotations embodied in critical reviews and certain other noncommercial uses permitted by copyright law.

Manufactured by Amazon.ca
Bolton, ON